DATE DUE

DE 1 2'00			
JV 24'00			
MY 0 9'07			
JE 2 9 0			
MR 2 7'09			

*First published in
the United States in 1991 by*
Gloucester Press
387 Park Avenue South
New York, NY 10016

Library of Congress Cataloging-in-Publication Data

Becklake, John.
    Food and farming / John and Sue Becklake.
        p.   cm. -- (Green issues)
    Includes index.
    Summary: Examines such recent issues surrounding food production
for the world's growing population as the benefits and problems of
fertilizers and pesticides, genetic engineering of crops, and
overproduction.
    ISBN 0-531-17288-0
    1. Agriculture--Juvenile literature. 2. Food supply--Juvenile
literature. [1. Food supply. 2. Agriculture.] I. Becklake, Sue.
II. Title. III. Series.
S519.B44   1991
630--dc20   90-45655   CIP   AC

Printed in Belgium

The publishers would like to acknowledge that
the photographs reproduced within this book
have been posed by models or have been
obtained from photographic agencies.

Design	David West
	Children's Book Design
Editor	Elise Bradbury
Picture Research	Emma Krikler
Illustrator	Rob Shone

*The author, Sue Becklake, has a degree in Science and
has written many books for children. This book was
written in collaboration with John Becklake.*

*The consultant, Brian Gardiner, is an atmospheric
scientist. He works for the British Antarctic Survey
and was one of the three scientists who discovered
the hole in the ozone layer.*

FOOD AND FARMING

**JOHN AND
SUE BECKLAKE**

GLOUCESTER PRESS
New York · London · Toronto · Sydney

CONTENTS

▷ In France the markets are filled with fresh fruit and vegetables from all over the world. However, millions of people in the developing countries do not have access to enough food to keep them healthy.

INTRODUCTION

Before the 20th century, if more food needed to be produced, more land needed to be cleared for farming. But in the last 50 years, with the help of machines, artificial fertilizers and pesticides, and improved strains of grain crops, farmers have been able to grow much more food on the same or even less land. The industrialized countries, for example, those in Europe and North America, have been able to grow more than enough food for everyone in spite of their expanding populations.

The story in the developing countries is very different. While some have benefited from advances in agriculture, many countries still have less food than they need, leaving millions permanently hungry and, as a result, vulnerable to disease. The populations in most of these regions have increased much faster than food production. Even where this is not the case, many people have neither access to farmland where they can grow their own produce, nor money to buy food. When there is a widespread famine, such as in Ethiopia in 1984, the world rallies around to send food to the starving. However, essential as famine relief is, it is not a long-term solution to food shortages. The answer is to help each country to grow and distribute food for its own people, while trying to control population growth.

Many of the techniques of modern farming are necessary to feed the world's growing population, but we must find ways to minimize the problems that often go with current farming practices. Overfarming wears out the soil, making it less productive and more liable to erosion. Pesticides and fertilizers pollute the environment. These and the other problems caused by intensive farming could ultimately damage our ability to supply enough food in the future for a rapidly growing population.

Chapter One

THE RISE OF MODERN FARMING

The world's population is growing by about 220,000 people every day and each one needs food to survive. To improve the efficiency of food production, farming has changed dramatically in this century. Scientists have bred new grain crops that yield more food per acre. Artificial fertilizers have encouraged growth, while pesticides have reduced crop loss from pests and diseases. The developed world's demand for meat has been met by the rearing of animals in large numbers. More of our food is processed (for example, frozen or canned) before we buy it. Some of these techniques are now spreading to parts of the developing world where more traditional farming methods have previously been the norm.

△ An efficient, modern farm in Israel

Population and food

Famines are not new. Throughout history societies have sometimes had problems growing enough food for everyone; the earliest recorded famines were in Egypt in about 3500 B.C. Famines were usually caused by natural disasters like floods or droughts, though wars often played a part, as they still do today. In 1798 an English economist called Thomas Malthus warned about the problems of feeding a growing population. He maintained that war, disease and famine were inevitable if population growth was not controlled. At that time there were less than one billion people in the world, but the population in Europe was beginning to increase fast. Now there are over five billion people in the world and the population is still expanding. In the past, people have been able to escape from long-term famine by migrating to less-populated areas of the world. However,

△ In the Soviet Union, lining up for food is common.

land suitable for agriculture is limited, so now farmers have to produce more food from the same amount of land. Since World War II, industrialized countries have concentrated on producing the maximum amount of food from the available farmland as cheaply and efficiently as possible. Encouragement has come in the form of government subsidies to farmers, guaranteeing them a good price for their products. Help has also come from scientists and the chemical industry, which supplies fertilizers and pesticides.

In the industrialized countries these efforts have been extremely successful because their populations have been growing more slowly, and now have more or less leveled off, particularly in Europe and North America. These countries grow plenty of food, with surpluses of certain products to store or export, and are rich enough to import many kinds of food from all over the world. But in many developing countries the number of people is growing much faster, and though the growth is beginning to slow down, the actual numbers will still be increasing well into the next century. In some areas food production has not kept up with the population explosion, and as these countries are often too poor to be able to import much food, some people never have enough to eat. Even where food production has grown as fast as the population, other factors, such as wars, can upset the distribution system. So even in these days of advanced mechanized farming in the industrialized parts of the world, we still sometimes see on our television screens the tragedy of a modern, avoidable famine.

Machines on the farm
Perhaps the most obvious difference between a modern farm in one of the

5

△ Harvest time in the United States

industrialized countries today and a farm of the past is the lack of people working there. Over the last century, mechanization has dominated on farms. Gradually people and work-animals have been replaced by machinery. Tractors have taken over the jobs previously done by horses. Tractors provide power for a wide variety of machines that prepare the land for planting and can sow and harvest the crops quickly and efficiently. Before mechanization it took five people a whole day to harvest two and a half acres; now one worker can harvest 50 acres in a day.

Mechanization has increased efficiency and reduced the amount the farmer has to pay workers, though large sums of money, often borrowed, must be spent on the machines and their upkeep. By specializing in a few crops or animals, a farmer becomes reliant on certain machines. However, an even wider variety of machines is necessary for mixed farming, where all kinds of food,

from cereal crops to milk, meat and eggs, are produced.

Machines in the food industry are not restricted to farms. Storage and transportation have become essential in delivering the farm product to the consumer and, while most deliveries are local, some food travels to customers in distant countries.

Chemical help

As plants grow they absorb materials they need from the soil. In fertile soil these are slowly replaced by natural processes like the rotting of animal or vegetable material. Planting different crops each season also replenishes the soil as each species takes in and puts back different nutrients. But natural processes are too slow for farmers who want to grow the same crop year after year on the same soil. Some farmers use natural methods and let the land recover, adding manure to help replace essential nutrients. However, since the 1950s, the chemical industry has aided farmers enormously by supplying artificial fertilizers containing the correct amounts of the chemicals needed for plants to grow well. Now the same kind of crop can be grown every year by feeding it with fertilizers, and modern varieties of cereal crop respond by producing more grain.

The chemical industry has also supplied farmers with other manufactured chemicals to protect crops. Pesticides include a wide range of different chemicals designed to kill insect pests (insecticides), weeds (herbicides) and fungal diseases (fungicides). Pesticides protect the crops during growth and also after they are harvested so they can be stored with the minimum of losses. Enormous quantities of these chemicals are now used on farms. Between 1950 and 1985, fertilizer use worldwide increased ninefold and the use of pesticides and similar chemicals 32-fold.

Veterinary drugs are also widely used to keep farm animals healthy. When large numbers of farm animals are kept together in a confined space, antibiotics are essential to prevent diseases spreading throughout the herd. Other drugs are used as well, like hormones, which are produced naturally in all animals but can also be made artificially. Hormones cause animals to gain weight and make cows produce more milk, but most are illegal on the grounds of safety. Consuming hormones in our food can have dangerous effects on our health, and many people are opposed to their use.

Meat and fish
In the last 30 years chicken has changed from a luxury food eaten only on special occasions to one of the cheapest meats available today. This has happened because of intensive farming – keeping huge numbers of animals in buildings called broiler houses. Here the temperature and lighting are controlled and the birds are fed the correct diet automatically. In this way an average roasting chicken can be produced in only 11 to 12 weeks. Hens can also be kept for egg production in laying houses. Under artificial light the hens are persuaded to lay all year around, while the eggs are collected automatically from the cages. These factory farming methods ensure a plentiful supply of cheap eggs and chickens. Pigs and calves are also raised intensively in units of thousands of animals, producing pork and veal quickly and efficiently. But these intensive farming methods form only a part of meat production. As the demand for meat increases, more and more land is cleared around the world for cattle ranching.

Another method of producing food that has become more widespread in recent years is fish farming, which produces fish like salmon and trout, as well as shellfish. Worldwide yields from aquaculture (fish

△ Chickens kept in laying houses produce eggs quickly and cheaply.

7

farming) tripled in the 1970s and are now 10 percent of world fish production. The United Nations would like to see a five- to tenfold increase in fish farming by the year 2,000, but this would mean a major change from small, local fish farms to expensive, large-scale developments.

The Green Revolution

In the years after World War II, dramatic increases in yields of cereal crops for human consumption (mainly wheat, corn and rice), and grasses for grazing animals, were seen as a revolution in food production. This "Green Revolution" was made possible by a combination of factors: the breeding of new varieties of grain, improved irrigation and wider use of fertilizers and pesticides.

These new farming methods were first launched in the industrialized world in the 1940s. Then, in the 1960s, they were introduced to parts of the developing world. Here it was hoped that the new cereal strains, cultivated with chemical help, would solve the increasing problem of providing food for the growing populations, and indeed the results were amazing. In India and Pakistan the wheat yields have

doubled, as have the rice outputs in Asia in general. Overall, in the 35 years between 1950 and 1985, world cereal production increased from about 650 million tons to about 1.8 billion tons: even faster than the population. We are now growing more food per person than in the 1950s, and on a smaller area of land.

Processing food

Much of the food we grow is processed, which means changed in some way, before we buy it. Food processing has been practiced for thousands of years, in one form or another, but it is now an increasing trend in most industrialized countries.

Although modern transportation can bring us food from anywhere in the world, at a cost, we still need to preserve food. The most common methods now are canning and freezing, which allow food to be kept for weeks, months or even years. One of the latest experimental methods of extending the useful life of some types of fresh food is to expose them to carefully controlled doses of radiation which kill the pests and diseases that would otherwise spoil the food.

Preserving is not the only reason for

△ Food processing includes canning and freezing which preserve food.

△ Huge dams, like this one in Brazil, supply electricity and can provide water for crops.

processing food. The busy lifestyle of many people leaves little time for preparing and cooking elaborate meals. More and more families buy meals that are ready-made or half-cooked and only need heating. Here again the chemical industry has helped food manufacturers by supplying "additives." These are chemicals added to food to prevent it from spoiling, or to enhance its color or flavor, both of which can suffer during processing. The result of all this processing is that supermarkets are stocked with a huge variety of all kinds of food throughout the year.

Progress in developing countries

Most of the rapid progress in farming and food production has happened in the wealthy, industrialized countries where food shortages are virtually unknown. However, even here some people are too poor to buy the right foods for a healthy, balanced diet.

In developing countries, advances in the form of the Green Revolution have only reached the wealthier landowners in the more fertile areas. They are the only people with enough money to buy the chemicals needed to grow the new cereal varieties. In Africa, Asia and South America, many families farm a small plot of land to grow enough food for themselves. The work is mostly done by manual labor, often by women using hand tools. In these areas the introduction of farm machines is not always appropriate. Only the wealthier farms are large enough to afford machines, and highly skilled workers are required to run them.

The development of irrigation projects has also been an essential part of agricultural development all over the world. The irrigation water in many cases is supplied by huge new dams. The area of irrigated land worldwide more than doubled between 1950 and 1985, and up to 30 percent of the world's food is grown on irrigated land. The agricultural progress seen in the last 50 years in the industrialized countries needs to be adapted to the conditions in the developing countries before it can help the poorest farmers to feed themselves.

The food we need

Food is the basic fuel for the human body, providing us with the energy to keep our bodies working. Many people do not get enough food and without it they do not have the energy to work. Malnutrition also affects the body's ability to cope with diseases. On the other hand, too much food can make a person fat and can contribute to heart disease, which is a major killer in industrialized countries. Heart disease affects 21 percent of American men in their fifties.

A healthy diet

To keep healthy, protein from lean meat, fish, eggs or beans is needed for growth. Fats from butter, cheese or meat supply energy, but carbohydrates from bread and cereals are a healthier source of energy. We also need vitamins and minerals. Roughage, or fiber, from fruit and vegetables keeps the digestive system healthy.

CARBOHYDRATE   FAT   PROTEIN   ROUGHAGE

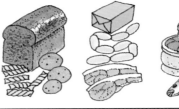

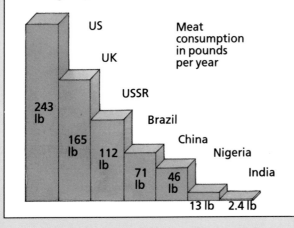

Diet in the industrialized countries

Diet in the developing world

Meat consumption

Meat is the major source of protein for most people in industrialized countries, although too much meat is not good for you. However, some people, like Eskimos, survive on a diet almost entirely of fish and meat, while vegetarians are quite healthy without eating any meat.

US

UK

USSR

Brazil

China

Nigeria

India

Meat consumption in pounds per year

243 lb

165 lb

112 lb

71 lb

46 lb

13 lb   2.4 lb

Different diets

In many developing countries, people eat a more monotonous and less healthy diet than most eat in industrialized countries. It is often lacking in protein and vitamins.

△ The average diet in the industrialized countries provides more than enough calories to stay healthy.

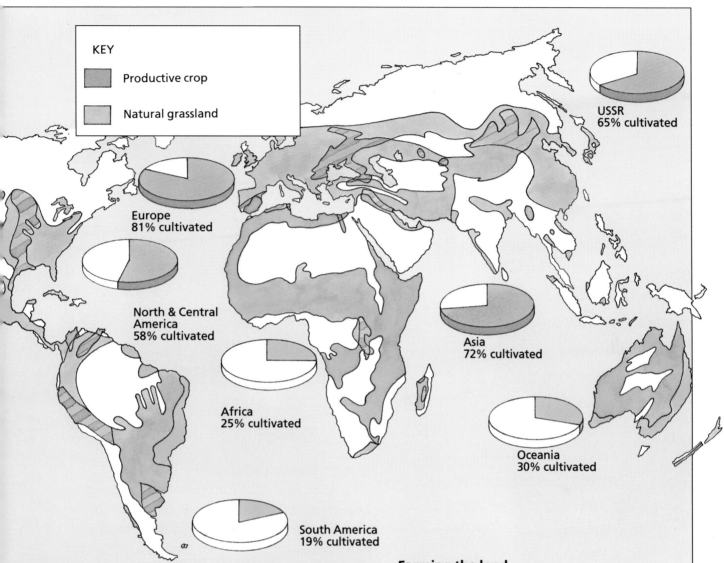

KEY

Productive crop

Natural grassland

USSR
65% cultivated

Europe
81% cultivated

North & Central
America
58% cultivated

Asia
72% cultivated

Africa
25% cultivated

Oceania
30% cultivated

South America
19% cultivated

Farming the land

In Europe and Asia most of the available farmland is put to good use, but not in Africa and South America. They have large stretches of grassland, but less than a quarter of the potential crop-growing land is now used for that purpose. This is one reason why many people there go hungry.

Energy from food

Our bodies convert much of the food we eat into energy, which is measured in calories. An average adult needs about 2,400 calories every day. In the industrialized countries, people get on average 37 percent more than they need, while about one in ten people in the world get less than 1,500 calories and suffer from malnutrition.

△ The average calorie intake of adults in the developing world is only 2,200 calories a day.

11

Chapter Two

PROBLEMS WITH AGRICULTURAL PROGRESS

Agricultural progress has enabled food production to keep up with the growing population in recent years. But new methods have often been adopted enthusiastically with little thought for their long-term effects, and there are many drawbacks. Pesticides and fertilizers escape from farms to pollute the environment. Overuse and misuse of farmland and forests result in soil erosion as valuable land is blown or washed away. Overfishing has reduced the numbers of some kinds of fish in the sea to such low levels that they may never fully recover. Much of our food now contains chemicals deliberately added during processing, as well as minute amounts of chemical pesticides and fertilizers.

△ Overgrazing can cause soil erosion.

Disappearing farmland

The basic essential for growing food crops and grazing animals is fertile soil. It can take thousands of years to build up soil good enough for farming, and scientists do not know of any shortcuts. However, it is much easier to destroy. Every year billions of tons of soil are eroded, blown away by the wind or washed away by rain, ending up at the bottom of lakes or oceans. In natural conditions, materials taken from the soil by growing plants are replaced gradually by manure and dead vegetation which are broken down by bacteria in the soil.

Creatures like ants and earthworms also help to maintain the structure of the soil by mixing it up, allowing air and moisture into it. Chemical fertilizers merely replace the chemicals used by the plants. They allow the soil to be used continuously, and under this stress the soil suffers, losing its structure and turning to dust. If windbreaks like bushes and trees, whose

△ Pesticides sprayed on these peas pollute the environment and can poison wildlife.

roots hold the soil together, are removed, there is little to stop the wind and rain from eroding the dusty soil. Tractors press down the soil so, instead of soaking in, rain runs off farmland, taking soil with it. Also, careless overwatering and farming on steep hillsides increase soil erosion. Soil losses are now enormous. Worldwide, 24 billion tons of topsoil are lost each year. In the United States, 4 billion tons of topsoil are lost every year – five tons of topsoil for every ton of corn that is produced. In hot, dry areas, the land is much more fragile and cannot easily recover from overuse, eventually turning into desert.

Often, good, productive farmland is lost when houses, factories, cities, roads and parking lots are built on it. In the United States, 12 square miles of land are covered by concrete every day, and the people who live and work in the new buildings rely on the decreasing farmland that remains to supply them with food.

Pollution from farming

The chemicals that help farmers to increase efficiency not only exhaust the soil, but also pollute the environment. Pesticides are all essentially poisons since they are designed to kill weeds, pests or diseases. They must always be handled very carefully; with some types it is necessary to wear protective clothing when using them. It is estimated that there are 20,000 deaths every year worldwide from pesticide poisonings. Many of these are in developing countries where handling instructions may not be understood or protective equipment is not available. Pesticides are usually applied by spraying, which is not a very efficient way of getting to the pest. In the United States 99 percent of all crops are sprayed with pesticides, often many times. In 1982, one lettuce crop in Britain was sprayed 46 times with four different pesticides! Spraying leaves excess chemicals to filter down through the soil into rivers and underground reservoirs and therefore into our water supplies. Minute amounts often remain in the crops which we ultimately consume as food. There are regulations to control the use of these chemicals, and crops are not harvested immediately after being sprayed, but it would be impossible to remove all traces of pesticides. Obviously it is illegal to sell food containing enough to poison people, but no one really knows the long-term effects of minute traces or of combinations of different chemicals in food.

Some of the early pesticides like DDT and dieldrin were very effective pest-killers and also very persistent. Instead of breaking down into other substances in the environment, they remained as pollutants for a very long time. They stayed in the bodies of insects and animals, becoming more concentrated higher up the food chain as larger creatures ate smaller ones. These persistent pesticides are now banned in many industrialized countries, but are sometimes exported to developing countries where they are still widely used. They may also find their way back to the exporting

country in imported food.

Pesticide use worldwide has increased enormously in the last 40 years and is not likely to decrease in the near future, because farmers often find they have to use increasing amounts. One reason is that insecticides kill the natural predators that help control the pests.

Fertilizers are not poisons but plant foods. The problem with them is that not all of the fertilizer is used by the plants. The rest is washed down through the soil by rain and filters into water supplies which then become polluted. Clean water supplied to many homes in industrialized countries contains an unsafe level of nitrates from fertilizers. In lakes and rivers the excess fertilizer makes the water plants grow too vigorously. They then die and decompose, using up all the oxygen in the water, and leaving it virtually lifeless.

Pests and diseases
Agricultural chemicals have caused a number of problems, which makes them less satisfactory than they seemed at first.

△ Without pesticides, pests could devastate this vast field of oats in Australia.

Fertilizers have enabled farmers to grow the same crops year after year on the same land and over huge areas. Growth of one crop, called monoculture, is seen in the grain belts of the United States and the Soviet Union, where the wheatfields stretch as far as the eye can see. This farming method provides a paradise for the pests and diseases which attack that crop because it ensures that a plentiful supply of their food is regularly available. Diseases can spread rapidly across a whole region causing huge crop losses, unless controlled by pesticides. This particularly affects the new Green Revolution varieties of grain because they are less resistant than traditional varieties which have evolved over the centuries to withstand diseases. Pests are not easily eliminated because they may become resistant to pesticides over a period of time. Farmers then need to use a larger amount of pesticides or rely on scientists to produce new pesticides to keep one step ahead of the pests. At least 428 insects have developed resistance to one pesticide or another, and houseflies and mosquitoes have overcome the poisoning effects of almost all of the chemicals used against them.

Animal prisons

The battle to produce meat cheaply and efficiently has led some farmers to use factory methods and treat their animals and poultry as meat- or egg-producing machines. Chickens, turkeys, pigs and calves are kept inside, often in the dark, in cages or pens only just big enough to hold them. Pigs can only stand or lie; they cannot turn around. Chickens, often five to a cage, with only four inches of cage-width each, are unable to stretch or flap their wings. Given the right food, they grow rapidly and provide meat or eggs very efficiently, but their conditions are far from natural and this often results in unnatural behavior like aggressiveness.

Animals bred to be kept in these conditions are also very prone to disease. With thousands living packed together in enclosed buildings, disease can easily spread through the whole unit. Antibiotics are used to prevent this, but, like pests, the

△ Pigs kept in intensive units spend their lives indoors.

diseases are not easily defeated. Some have adapted to become resistant to certain antibiotics. This can become a danger to human health. Recently, salmonella food poisoning, caused by bacteria, has increased rapidly. In rare cases it can be fatal. Usually it can be cured by antibiotics, but now there are strains that are resistant to some antibiotics. This resistance may well have developed through the overuse of antibiotics in intensive farming, limiting their usefulness in curing humans.

Many people, including some farmers, oppose these factory methods. And those who do adopt factory farming are caught in a vicious circle. The more efficient they are at producing meat, the more there is on the market and so the cheaper the price. But the costs of feedstuffs, heating, lighting, medicines and veterinary bills tend to go up rather than down, and to meet these expenses they must produce even more to sell, perpetuating these questionable methods of keeping animals.

Overgrazing and overfishing

Animals on the land can cause problems if there are so many of them that they eat the grass and plantlife faster than it can grow. In fertile areas land can be made to support more animals if fertilizers are used to make the grass grow faster, though in the long run the soil suffers. On more fragile land, particularly in dry, tropical areas, plantlife will only recover if the animals are moved on regularly to graze different areas, as in the traditional nomadic way of life. If not, the soil loses its protective cover of plants, which leads to erosion, and eventually the area may become barren desert.

We are also succeeding in turning the oceans into deserts. When we consider that two-thirds of the world's surface is water, we might imagine that the oceans could provide an inexhaustible supply of fish, but this is not so. To maintain a supply of fish it

△ Overfishing leaves nothing for the future.

is necessary to leave enough in the sea to breed and produce future generations. This has not happened in the last 40 years. Fishing has become much more efficient, with fleets of larger ships and factory ships that freeze the fish or turn it into animal feed or fertilizers as soon as it is caught. Between 1950 and 1970 fish harvests increased by six to seven percent per year, much faster than population growth and even faster than the grain yields from the new Green Revolution strains. In the North Atlantic, herring has been fished almost to extinction and cod and haddock have become increasingly rare. Overfishing has also occurred in the Pacific and the South Atlantic, and the situation is not helped by pollution, which also reduces the numbers of fish in some places. The industrialized nations have reacted by sending their

△ BSE can cause cows to act strangely.

fishing fleets further afield to the rich fishing areas of the Southern Hemisphere, where they deplete the fish stocks.

Poisons in our food

In addition to the traces of pesticides and fertilizers that contaminate some of the food we consume, another increasing problem is food poisoning, which is caused by harmful bacteria. These bacteria are killed by thorough cooking, but the increasing trend of buying precooked food to heat at home provides ideal conditions for bacteria to multiply to dangerous levels. Salmonella bacteria, which occur in poultry, meat and eggs, caused at least 50,000 cases of food poisoning in the United States in 1987, as compared to about 30,000 in 1978. It is probably spread to animals by giving them infected feed.

BSE (bovine spongiform encephalopathy), which caused a food scare in Britain in 1990 under the name of "mad cow disease," is also thought to be spread by infected animal feed. It is a brain disease in cows which seems to have come from sheep. It only appeared after farmers started giving their cows feed containing remains of sheep, which may have died from a similar disease. It is still unknown whether or not it could spread to humans through infected beef. After an outcry in the press the government decided to compensate farmers for cows that had to be destroyed because of BSE, so infected carcasses were no longer sold for meat. Both salmonella and BSE seem to have been caused by feeding methods which could be better regulated.

There are also doubts about the safety of using radiation to preserve food, though it is permitted in some countries for certain foods like pork, and some spices and vegetables. The radiation does not remain in the food, it just kills insects and bacteria that spoil the food or cause food poisoning. It also delays ripening, making fruit and vegetables look fresh for longer. It is very useful to the food trade, allowing food to be stored longer before it is sold. Stored grain can also be treated with radiation to kill pests that would spoil it, reducing losses which can be costly. However, radiation does cause chemical changes in food, and it is too early to say what long-term effects these may have on people's health.

Additives – are they all bad?

Many substances are added to food during processing. Anything that is put into food before we buy it is called an additive. This includes vitamins and minerals like calcium and iron which are all essential to health. Vitamins are often added to replace those lost from the original food during processing. Preservatives, which slow down the rate at which food spoils, are also important additives. Without them we have to be very careful to store food correctly and to use it before it goes bad, or it may cause food poisoning.

However, there is a large group of nonessential additives that are added just to make food attractive by enhancing its color or flavor or altering its texture. Therefore, the term "food additives" can be used for any nonfood substance added to food during processing to improve the food's color, flavoring, texture, or nutritional

△ Foods we enjoy, such as chocolates, have many additives.

value. There are many thousands of additives. In the United States, the Food and Drug Administration (FDA) has classified those additives used before 1958 with no reported harmful effects as Generally Regarded as Safe, often abbreviated GRAS. After 1958 the FDA began testing all additives before approving their use, and since 1970 has begun reviewing some of those on the old GRAS list. As a result of these investigations, cyclamate, an artifical sweetener, has been banned; the use of saccharin limited; and various dyes and other agents put under intensive laboratory analysis. In one highly publicized event, the FDA banned the use of Red Dye # 2. This dye was replaced by Red Dye # 40, which is banned in Great Britain, Canada, and some other countries.

Food surpluses
The production of too much food happens when farmers are guaranteed a minimum price for their produce whether the public wants to buy it or not, as in Europe and the United States. The extra that cannot be sold in the marketplace is bought by the government. In the United States, as well as in the European Community, huge surpluses are stored – and sometimes wasted. These guaranteed prices encourage farmers to produce as much as possible without regard for the long-term damage to the soil.

△ These surplus apples from European countries are just dumped and left to rot.

Farming: bad and good

Agricultural advances have succeeded in supplying us with all kinds of food. However, many of the methods used in modern farming are not sustainable. They damage the land so that it cannot continue to produce good crops indefinitely. In addition they are expensive. For these reasons, more farmers should adopt practices which would ensure yields into the future.

Intensive animal units

Animals kept together in large numbers produce an enormous amount of waste. If they are kept indoors their manure is usually dumped in slurry pits which may leak, polluting rivers.

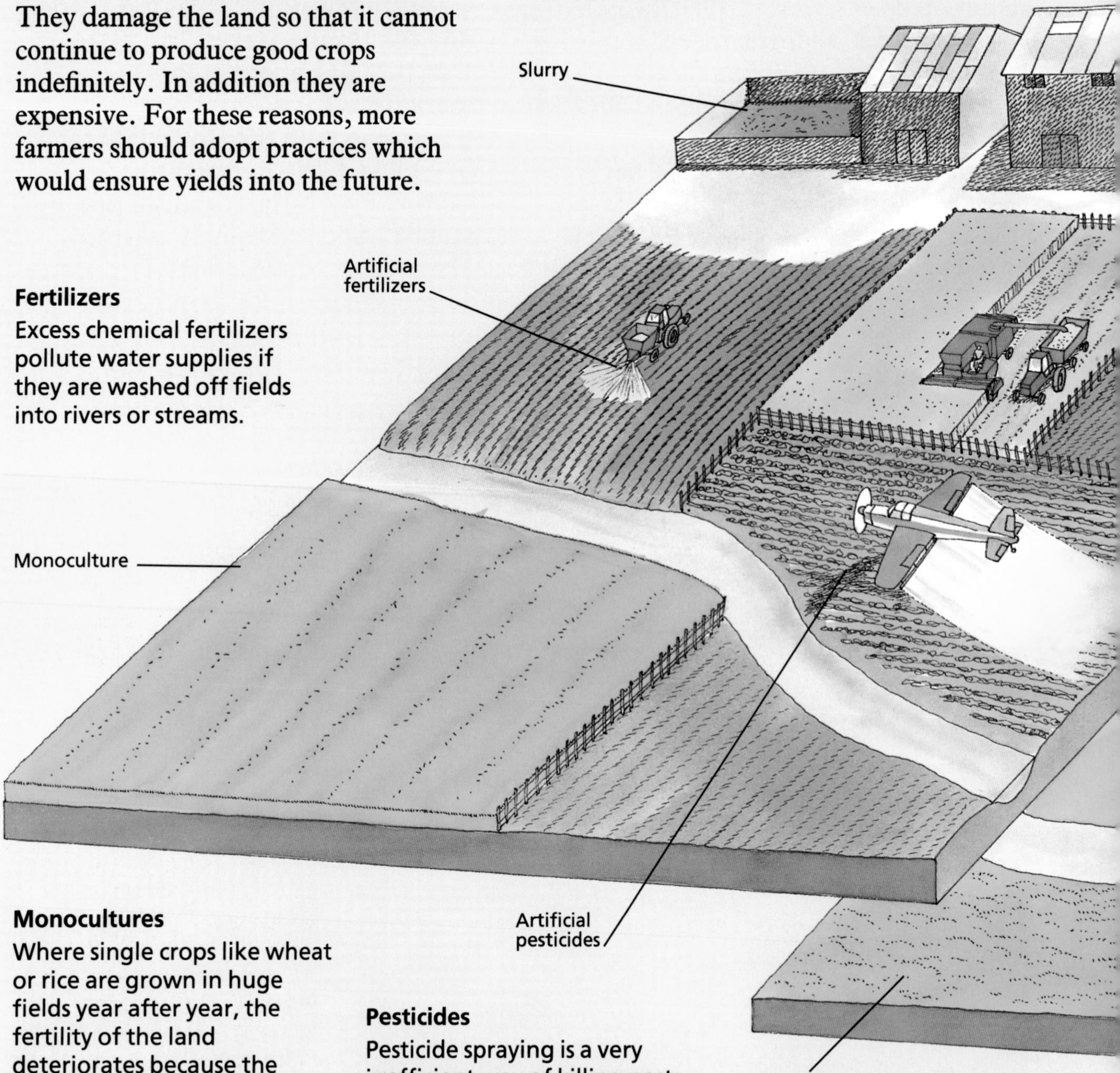

Slurry

Artificial fertilizers

Fertilizers

Excess chemical fertilizers pollute water supplies if they are washed off fields into rivers or streams.

Monoculture

Artificial pesticides

Land left fallow

Monocultures

Where single crops like wheat or rice are grown in huge fields year after year, the fertility of the land deteriorates because the plants sap all the nutrients from the soil. To accommodate machines, the fields have no trees and hedges which would protect the soil from erosion by wind and rain.

Pesticides

Pesticide spraying is a very inefficient way of killing pests. Very little actually hits its target, and it also kills the insects that control pests. Traces of pesticides now contaminate much of our food and our water supplies.

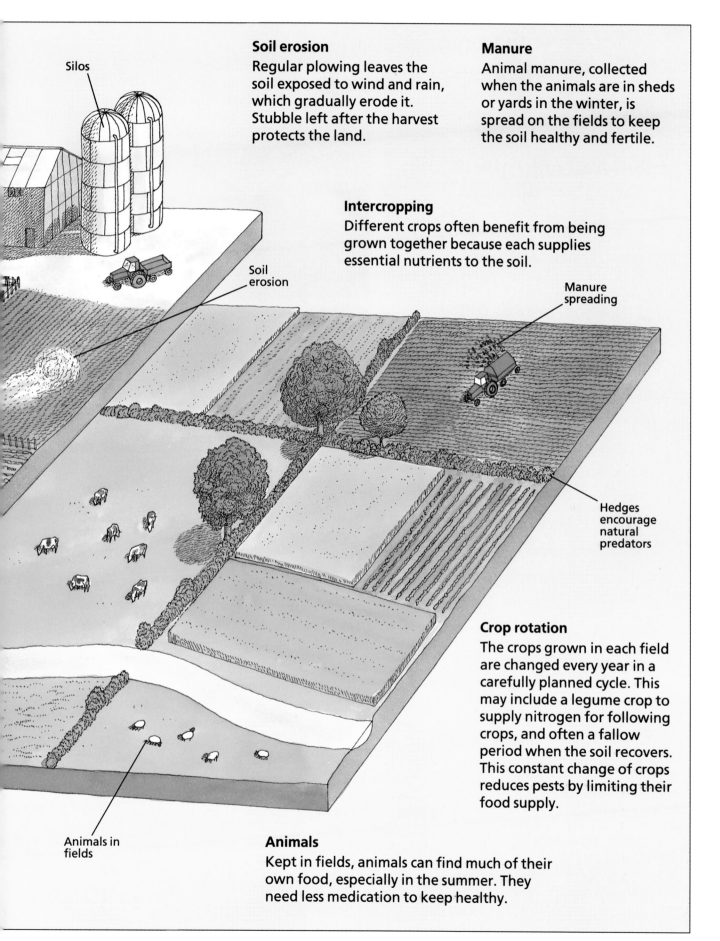

Silos

Soil erosion
Regular plowing leaves the soil exposed to wind and rain, which gradually erode it. Stubble left after the harvest protects the land.

Manure
Animal manure, collected when the animals are in sheds or yards in the winter, is spread on the fields to keep the soil healthy and fertile.

Intercropping
Different crops often benefit from being grown together because each supplies essential nutrients to the soil.

Soil erosion

Manure spreading

Hedges encourage natural predators

Crop rotation
The crops grown in each field are changed every year in a carefully planned cycle. This may include a legume crop to supply nitrogen for following crops, and often a fallow period when the soil recovers. This constant change of crops reduces pests by limiting their food supply.

Animals in fields

Animals
Kept in fields, animals can find much of their own food, especially in the summer. They need less medication to keep healthy.

21

Chapter Three

FOOD AND FARMING IN THE DEVELOPING WORLD

In the developing countries, farmers' problems are often more difficult to solve than those of farmers in the industrialized nations. The weather and the soil in some tropical countries can make it much harder to grow food efficiently. Also, the populations there have been expanding very fast, defeating the efforts of the people to feed themselves. Many try to farm fragile, semidesert areas or cut down the forests for farmland, but this is only a temporary answer. Irrigation can help but it must be used carefully so it does not damage the soil. Many countries have debts which have to be repaid. To earn the money for this they grow crops for export on land where food could be grown to feed their people.

△ Many Africans get water from wells.

Different ways of farming

The farming areas of most of the industrialized countries lie between the equator and the poles, in those regions with a temperate climate. There is plenty of rain and the right temperatures to grow a wide variety of produce. The seasons provide a cold winter, killing off many pests, and a hot summer that ripens the crops. The main crops are potatoes, sugar beet and cereals, including wheat, barley and, in warmer places, corn. Large areas of land are also used to grow food for animals since meat makes up a large part of the diet in the industrialized countries.

The picture is very different in most of the developing countries, which in general have much hotter, drier climates. The rainfall may come only during the rainy season, leaving the rest of the year very dry. Wheat is grown in India and the Far East, and corn in Africa. However, in general,

United Nations Food and Agriculture Organization estimates that up to 30 percent of food is lost in storage in the developing countries, and the new Green Revolution varieties of grain seem to be particularly vulnerable.

The Green Revolution has greatly increased food production in Asia, where rice and wheat farmers have benefited from the higher productivity of the new varieties. China and India now produce enough rice and wheat to feed their populations. However, the Green Revolution has not helped in drier areas; Africa is the only region in the world where the food supply per person has decreased since 1970.

Population pressure

Despite efforts to control it, the population of the whole world is still increasing. The total population was five billion in 1987 and will reach six billion before the year 2000. Most of this increase will be in the developing countries, particularly Africa and the Middle East where food is already in short supply. There are thought to be about 500 million people, one-tenth of the world's population, without enough food to stay healthy. Every year some 40 million people die of hunger, infections or diseases caused by malnutrition.

Malnutrition hits hardest at children, who are not strong enough to survive childhood diseases without adequate food. If they do survive, they do not grow and develop as they normally should. According to one report, 53 percent of children in Ghana suffer from malnutrition, and the number of infant deaths there is rising.

In their efforts to grow enough food for their families, people are often forced to farm poor, semidesert land. This land is so fragile that it can only support crops or herds of animals for a short while before it is exhausted. Then it eventually becomes desert. This is known as desertification, and

rice is a much more important crop in Asia. In the drier parts of Africa and the Middle East the main crops are cassava, a root crop, and a cereal called sorghum – both of which can resist drought. Relatively few animals are raised for meat, and fish is more important than meat in the diet. Many more people work on the land than is the case in the industrialized countries. In Indonesia, 80 percent of the people work in food production and 70 percent of Africans are subsistence farmers, meaning they grow crops from a small plot of land to supply food only for their own families.

In these hot climates with no cold winters many pests and diseases thrive. In some areas locusts pose a severe threat to crops. A large swarm of locusts can destroy 80,000 tons of food in a day, enough to feed 400,000 people for a year! Pests are not only a problem while crops are growing, they also spoil or destroy stored food. The

the area of land lost in this way each year is estimated to be almost twice the size of Belgium. However, desertification is not irreversible; some schemes have been successful in making semidesert land able to sustain crops.

If it becomes too difficult to make a living from the land, many people migrate to the cities in the hope of finding a job. The cities become surrounded by shanty towns, which often spring up on good land that could be used for farming. Half the population of Latin America now lives in cities, the majority in shanty towns. The city-dwellers cannot grow their own food so they rely on farmers to supply them from the dwindling amount of farmland.

Destroying the forests
Pressure to extend farmland may also drive people to destroy the forests and woods. The tropical forests of South America, Africa and Asia are very rich in the variety of life they support, and if used carefully

they can supply many valuable materials. The rainforests were the original sources of many of today's valuable crops like tea, coffee, sugar, rice and corn, among others. Also, many modern medicines have ingredients derived from rainforest species. Forests affect the local and even the global climate, increasing rainfall by releasing moisture from the trees, and reducing flooding by absorbing water like a sponge. However, there are very few nutrients in the soil, and it is not at all suitable for farming. After a few years of being used for cattle grazing it is exhausted. Traditionally, the South American Indians would clear small plots by cutting and burning the forest, farm for a few years and then move on. This method left seeds and some nutrients in the ground, and the forest gradually grew back, taking about 100 years to return to its former state. Today, machines completely clear huge areas very quickly to provide grazing and farmland. In about five to eight years what little goodness

△ Shanty towns, like this one on the outskirts of Hong Kong, leave no land to grow food.

24

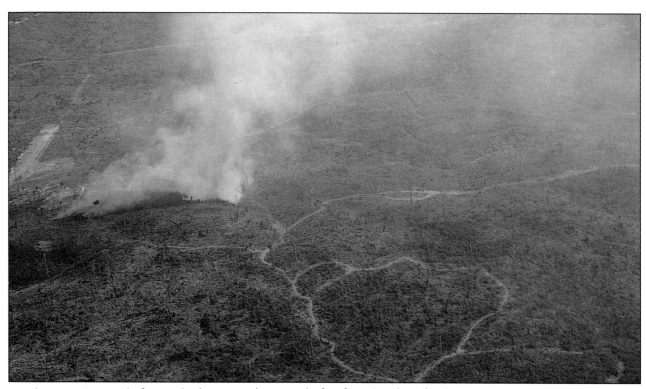

△ The Amazon rainforest is destroyed not only for farming but for large-scale ranching as well.

there was in the soil is used up, the forest cannot reestablish itself, and only useless scrubland is left. Nearly half of all tropical forests have already been destroyed, with almost none at all left in India, Bangladesh and Sri Lanka, and if anything, this destruction is accelerating. Over a quarter of the Central American rainforest has been destroyed since 1960.

Another reason for cutting down forests, especially in Africa, is for firewood. About two billion people rely on firewood for all their cooking and heating. The expanding populations are using up the wood faster than the trees can grow, but these people have no other choice.

Famine and food aid
One result of destroying forests is a drier climate, since the forest trees release water vapor into the air, contributing to rainfall. Forest destruction may have been one of the causes of the droughts and tragic famines that swept Africa in the 1980s. Droughts and floods can both cause complete crop failure, but this should not lead to widespread famine unless harvests repeatedly fail or there is some other reason why people cannot get food from elsewhere. That reason may be extreme poverty but often it is war, which can drive people from their land or prevent food from being transported to where it is needed. When the situation gets really desperate, people finally have to leave their homes and land to take their children to towns or emergency relief centers, where food might be available.

When news of the famine reaches the television screens of the rich, industrialized nations of the North, many people give money generously to send food, but this arrives too late for many of the starving. It takes time to organize emergency food aid, ship it to the nearest port and then transport it thousands of miles to the famine areas. This will only work with the agreement of all the governments involved, a major problem in war-torn areas. Another problem is ensuring that the food gets to the people it is intended for. During the

African famine of 1984 many countries sent food aid to Ethiopia, but some arrived over a year after it was promised. That famine affected 150 million people.

While emergency food aid is essential once widespread famine has occurred, it is only a partial measure. People need help before they get so desperate that they have to leave their homes. Otherwise they will not be able to prepare the land and sow the seed for next year's harvest and there will be no food again in following years.

Is all aid helpful?

While emergency aid is perhaps the most obvious kind of help sent from the industrialized countries to the developing world, there are also other kinds. It can be direct food aid, such as giving people food in exchange for work, or assistance with major projects aimed at developing industry and modernizing agriculture. However, many of these attempts to help, especially those from governments and large international organizations, do not reach the poorest people. The Green Revolution projects resulting in increased grain yields for the richer farmers often leave the poorer ones worse off, as they are forced to leave or sell their land. Projects like dam building, which look good on paper, disrupt large areas and again may result in smaller farmers having to leave their land.

Even food aid has its drawbacks. If cheap food becomes available, the local farmers cannot get a good price for their crops and so they produce less food for sale. Local food supply problems increase and the country becomes more dependent on aid when it could be growing more of its own food. Also, much aid has strings attached; it is given on condition that the receiving country buys goods from the country sending the aid. Many industrialized nations only give aid to developing countries with certain governments. Even though it is very poor, Ethiopia receives less aid per person than many other African countries because its government is not approved of by Western governments.

△ Emergency aid supplies milk to feed a child.

△ Many people worldwide depend on aid.

26

Cash crops and debt

Huge areas of good farmland in developing countries now grow cash crops instead of food for the local population. Cash crops are products like tea, coffee, sugar, and cotton that are grown for export, mainly to the industrialized countries. In West Africa 70 percent of the Gambia's and 55 percent of Senegal's arable land is used to grow peanuts for export. Crops like these are intended to earn money for the developing countries on the international markets and they are being grown on an increasing scale. In the last 25 years Africa's output of cotton and cocoa has doubled, sugar has tripled and coffee has quadrupled. In fact, Africa exports more food products than it imports, but it cannot feed its own population.

As well as raising money to pay for imports, cash crops are needed to pay interest on debts. In the 1970s many developing countries were offered loans from banks in the industrialized countries in order to develop their economies and thereby reduce poverty. The interest on the loans was to be paid by growing cash crops or selling natural resources. However, in the 1980s the interest rates rose sharply and it became impossible for the countries to pay the interest even by growing more cash crops. The interest rates have now risen so high that the developing countries are paying more in interest to the banks than they receive as aid. The International Monetary Fund will lend money but only after imposing conditions, including cutting services like health and education and reducing wages. The effect of this in countries where there is already extreme poverty is increased malnutrition and even starvation, especially among the young.

The trouble with relying on cash crops to earn an income is that prices on world markets are not fixed. If too much of any product is grown or if there is less demand for any reason, the price falls. In general, world prices have declined since 1950. This then creates a temptation to grow more cash crops, which will only depress the price further, causing more poverty.

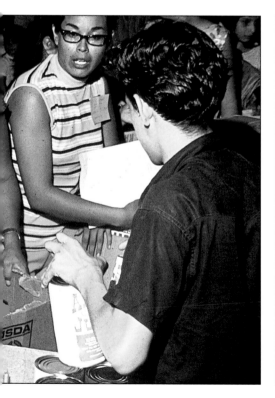

△ Tobacco is grown as a cash crop in Nigeria.

Irrigation

One way of growing more crops on very dry land is to use irrigation, which means supplying water to the plants through channels and sprinklers, or, in the case of rice, by flooding the fields. A farmer in a dry region of the United States can produce nearly three times a normal yield of corn just by watering the fields. About 15 percent of the world's croplands are now irrigated and they produce 30 percent of the world's food. In fact, irrigation accounts for almost three-quarters of the water used worldwide. So by using irrigation more widely we should be able to increase food production dramatically. However, there are problems with this, especially if irrigation is used continuously to produce crops year after year, or even several crops a year, without allowing the soil to recover.

All water and soils contain some salts which damage plants if they become too concentrated. In rainy areas these salts are regularly washed out of the soil, but in hot, dry regions there is less rainfall, which evaporates, leaving the land with more salts. When these soils are irrigated, the water in the ground rises, dissolving salts from the soil and bringing them up to the level of the plant roots. The land becomes waterlogged and water evaporates at the surface leaving the salts to damage the plants. This is called salinization. It is estimated that between 30 percent and 80 percent of all irrigated land suffers to some degree from waterlogging and salinization. Many countries, including Pakistan, Egypt and Peru, are affected, as is the United States. In the worst cases land can no longer be used to grow crops. The total area of land that has to be abandoned for this reason is possibly as great as that which is newly irrigated for food production.

There is also often a problem in supplying enough water for irrigation. Huge dams have been seen as an answer to this, especially since they also provide electricity, but they do have drawbacks. Dams can supply all the water needed, but the lake behind the dam covers a large area, often flooding farmland and uprooting thousands of people. Dams also trap the silt normally carried downstream by the river. The Nile River in Egypt regularly floods its valley. It used to deposit a layer of fertile silt on the land along its banks until the Aswan Dam was built. Now the fields are irrigated, but they do not benefit from the silt trapped behind the dam. Also, the sardine fishery as far away as the Mediterranean Sea has collapsed because it is deprived of the nutrients that the Nile carried down to it. The Aswan Dam has also caused an increase in waterborne diseases, since the lake provides perfect breeding grounds for malaria and cholera. In some areas near the Aswan Dam, whole communities are affected by this disease. Large projects like this often have negative side effects, but

△ Irrigating this orchard with sprinklers will help to produce more fruit.

small, local development schemes are usually much less damaging.

Traditional ways

Over the centuries people have learned which crops will grow in the soil and climate in their area, and how to survive without doing too much harm to the environment. There is nothing wrong with these traditional ways, but with populations growing fast in the developing countries, it has become necessary to grow more food. It is possible to introduce improvements to many of these traditional methods without harming the environment, combining local knowledge with the benefit of modern agricultural science.

However, some traditions make it difficult to introduce developments. In many communities the men are at the head of the family and are the main decision makers, but the women do most of the work in the fields. In Africa, over 70 percent of the agricultural work is done by women. Indeed the men may leave the villages to look for work in the towns, leaving the women on their own to provide food for the

△ Primitive plows are still used in Nepal.

family. Training projects are set up to teach new farming methods and improve efficiency but these are mainly attended by men, not the women who do the work. Progress is often very slow.

Other traditions may perpetuate poverty and hunger even when there should be plenty of food for all. This is true of many countries where severe inequality between rich and poor has not been solved. In 1985 the wheat harvest in India was so good that there was not enough room in the warehouses to store it all, but at the same time many people had to struggle to get food, some resorting to begging. The gulf between rich and poor is probably greatest in Latin America. In Brazil, as in India, the vast majority of the land is owned by a small minority of rich farmers. Both India and Brazil export more food than they import while many of the people do not have enough to eat. It seems that, with the exception of Africa, where 44 percent of the land is affected by drought, the problem is not growing enough food but sharing it more equally.

△ Brazilians grow coffee as a cash crop.

Chapter Four

THE WAY AHEAD

The world can produce enough food for all at present, but the population is continuing to increase, and will probably double in size before it levels off. Thus, eventually the world must be able to produce twice the present quantity of food if we are to avoid mass starvation. If the land suitable for farming is treated with great care, and we learn from our mistakes with chemical fertilizers and pesticides and careless irrigation, it may provide us with food year after year. A change in diet towards less meat would also help by releasing more land to grow crops for human consumption. Above all, we must make sure that everyone gets a share of the food that is grown.

△ Terraced fields protect soil from erosion.

Looking after the land

The first essential for food production is good soil, and this is in short supply. At present only about 11 percent of the earth's land surface is suitable for cultivation. It is estimated that about the same area again could be developed for farming, but it would be very expensive to do this. If we are to supply all our future food needs we must take good care of the farmland we have now.

The vast amount of soil lost through erosion can be reduced in many ways. Trees, bushes or even tough varieties of grass planted between crops will hold the soil together and reduce wind speed and wind erosion. Stubble will also protect the soil if it is left in the field after a harvest, instead of being plowed immediately. The next crop can then be sown in furrows cut through the stubble. Where hilly areas

to recover without growing crops – this is called lying fallow. This was a regular part of farming practice until it was reduced as a result of the use of chemical fertilizers and the pressure to grow more food. Plants called legumes, like peas and beans, and clover, enrich the soil with nitrogen, one of the most important requirements for healthy plant growth.

At present we do not always make the best use of the land we have. Although some regions like Europe and the Far East use almost all the land that is suitable for farming, this is not true worldwide. Both Africa and South America have unused land that could be developed for growing food. Careful irrigation can help drier parts of the world to bring more land into cultivation. Holland has increased its farmland by reclaiming land from the sea. However, many scientists fear that the increase in polluting gases from burning fossil fuels (like coal, gas and oil) is causing the world temperature to rise; a phenomenon known as global warming. This could cause the sea level to rise, flooding many acres of fertile land around coasts.

are farmed, the rain will not wash as much soil away if the hillsides are built up into steps, or terraces. Terraced paddy fields in the Philippines have produced rice crops for two thousand years.

The salinization and waterlogging that ruin irrigated land can be avoided, partly by making sure there is adequate drainage to prevent the buildup of water and salts. Trickle and drip irrigation techniques also help. This system uses pipes with holes that supply just enough water directly to the plants. This does not waste water and there is much less evaporation because only small areas of soil around the plants get wet.

Soil structure can also be maintained by adding animal manure or rotted plant material. Green manure, for example, clover, is a crop, which is grown just to be plowed back into the land to enrich the soil. It is also sometimes necessary to leave land

Farming without pollution
It is useless to grow plenty of food if it is dangerously contaminated with chemicals. Some farmers are now turning their backs on chemicals altogether and farming organically, which means they use no artificial fertilizers or pesticides at all. Instead they use natural fertilizers, including animal manure and rotting plant material, to enrich the soil. Pest damage can be reduced by several methods, for example crop rotation. This means that each field grows a different crop every year, usually in a four-year cycle, depriving the pests of a continuous supply of food. Putting different crops in each field not only limits the pests' food supply, but also the damage they can do. Natural predators help to

control insect pests, and an organic farm remains free from pollution. There are some losses from pest damage, resulting in lower yields than intensive farming produces, but the farmer does not have to buy chemicals, so costs are less. Unfortunately, the cost of organic produce to the consumer prohibits many from buying it, so farmers may be wary of growing it.

Sustainable farming, like organic farming, puts the emphasis on caring for the land to keep it fertile and able to produce food indefinitely. However, it does not rule out the use of chemicals when they are absolutely necessary. It aims to make the best use of good farmland, maximizing yields by growing a wide variety of crops without harming the soil.

Science can help

Agricultural scientists help the farmer by developing new strains of crops, investigating pests and looking for new sources of food. They have already bred grain varieties with much higher yields, but the early types had drawbacks. They were more easily damaged by pests, did not store as well as conventional varieties, and needed plenty of water and fertilizer to grow well. Scientists have improved the pest resistance of the new grains, but keeping ahead of pests is a never-ending task. They are now trying to breed useful qualities from one species of plant to another. The ability of legumes to use nitrogen from the air as plant food would be very useful if it could be transferred to other crops, reducing their need for nitrogen fertilizers. Some plants have a natural resistance to pests; for example, the hairy potato repels aphids (insect pests), and this natural pest control could protect crops if it could be bred into them.

Other pest controls include natural predators, which are insects that feed on the pests. Scientists can find suitable ones to attack a particular pest. Another approach is to interfere with the pests' breeding by creating sterile males that cannot produce offspring, thus decreasing their numbers. These methods all reduce the need for chemical pesticides.

Investigations into different plant species can reveal varieties that might become a valuable new source of food. One promising species is the winged bean, which grows in the tropics. Not only is it a legume, supplying its own nitrogen, but it is completely edible and could provide useful food in areas where other food crops are difficult to grow. Another useful potential food source is the Yeheb bush, a woody shrub that grows in hot, dry, semidesert areas and has large seeds that can be eaten by people or by grazing animals.

Sensible eating

There has been an increasing trend recently in the rich, industrialized countries to eat a higher proportion of meat: about six times as much meat as is eaten in the developing

▽ Ladybugs eat blackfly pests on bean plants.

countries. Meat can be an important part of a healthy diet, supplying the protein needed for growth, but it is not healthy to eat too much. In addition, meat is a very inefficient way of producing food – beef cattle use about 22 pounds of grain to provide just two pounds of meat. The world supports twice as many domestic animals as humans. These animals graze on almost half of the world's ice-free surface – four times the area that is cultivated for crop growing. Many grazing animals, for example, goats and some sheep, are able to survive on land that is too poor to be cultivated, putting it to good use. They convert grass and other plants that humans cannot eat into meat for our consumption. However, modern intensive rearing of chickens, pigs and cattle prevents them from finding their own food by grazing, and they have to be fed, largely on grain. In the United States, 75 percent of grain production goes to feed animals. These animals are eating huge quantities of food that humans could eat, in order to provide a much smaller amount of meat. If we ate less meat, the land that is cultivated for grain for animal feed could be planted to feed many more humans.

We could make more use of wild animals and those that have not been traditionally used for food. Farmers are now starting to raise deer to provide meat because they can graze on poorer pasture than cattle. In tropical countries it is sensible to use the local animals that are adapted to the climate and conditions instead of trying to raise cattle which are more suited to a cooler climate. Some livestock do not contribute to the food supply at all. India has one-sixth of the world's cattle but they are not killed and eaten because the Hindu religion forbids it. In many African countries cattle represent wealth rather than a source of food.

Protein can also come from sources other than meat. Some vegetables, particularly beans, contain a lot of protein, and scientists have processed these into synthetic meat. Many of us may have eaten "meat" made from soy beans. Scientists are also now using microscopic organisms, including fungi, to produce protein which can be manufactured into synthetic foods. Perhaps these will be the food of the future.

▽ Beef cattle in the United States are fed large amounts of grain.

Sharing equally

The food grown worldwide is very unevenly distributed at present, both within countries and between countries. Some people starve while others have enough food to waste. Inequality within countries has to be resolved by individual governments. Unfortunately, the poor often cannot read or write and their means for putting pressure on their governments are limited. The rich landowners are the people with the political power. China has achieved a level of equality in food distribution, but it took a revolution to do it.

There must also be international cooperation, instead of the present situation in which each government protects its own farmers by stopping imports that will compete with its products. The industrialized countries also buy and sell so much that they affect world prices with their trade. When buying and selling inter-nationally, the more developed nations need to have more consideration for the effects on the farmers of developing countries.

Education is also important in helping people to be self-sufficient. General education will give people more say in the government of their own countries, making sure that the poorest people are not neglected. The industrialized countries can help by teaching improved farming methods to the people who actually do the work, in many cases the women.

None of this will be of any use at all if the world's population growth does not stop. If it continues to grow there will come a time, no matter how many scientific advances are made, when the world can no longer feed everyone. Experts predict that if we control the growth, the population should level off at about 10 billion people sometime in the next century. It will be a struggle to feed all these people, but scientists believe we can do it. The industrialized and developing countries will have to work together, finding ways of using all the world's farmland to produce the maximum amount of food, and then sharing it so that there is enough for all.

△ Women from Mali bring in a good harvest.

China's success

China successfully feeds 22 percent of the world's population using only seven percent of the world's farmland. To do this it has the largest irrigation network in the world and grows more than a third of the world's rice crop. Fish farming provides a very efficient source of protein. Most of the waste material is recycled into fertilizer or fish food. The waste from plants, animals and human sewage can also be useful in providing energy. The methane gas which is produced by the decay of waste can be burned for cooking and heating or for electricity.

GLOSSARY

additives chemicals added to food during processing.

aid help given to poor countries by rich ones, such as money, food or technical help.

antibiotics drugs used to cure illnesses in people and animals.

BSE (bovine spongiform encephalopathy) a fatal brain disease of cows.

cash crops agricultural products grown for sale abroad and not to provide food for the local people.

cereals plants that produce grain, including wheat, rice, corn and sorghum.

crop rotation changing crops from field to field, usually in a four-year cycle, so that each field grows a different crop each year.

desertification reducing dry, infertile land to desert through overuse, poor irrigation or cutting down forests.

developing countries poorer countries with little industry and mainly rural economies.

erosion loss of fertile soil due to the action of wind and rain, often increased by careless farming methods.

fallow land left without crops for a year or two to let it recover after cultivation.

fertilizer natural or artificial plant food which is added to the soil to increase plant growth.

Green Revolution agricultural advance which combined the development of new strains of wheat and rice that give much higher yields, with irrigation, pesticides and fertilizers. This resulted in a huge increase in food production.

industrialized countries richer countries where industry provides more jobs than agriculture.

irrigation supplying water to crops through pipes or channels or by spraying.

legumes plants that convert nitrogen from the air into a form that can be used as food for the plant.

malnutrition inadequate diet, usually from too little food, leading to disease and stunted growth.

monoculture growing large areas of the same crop in the same fields year after year.

natural predators creatures which eat insects and other pests that damage crops.

pesticides chemicals that kill insect pests, weeds or plant diseases.

pollution the release of harmful substances into the environment.

processing a range of techniques that prepare, preserve and package food before it is sold.

salinization concentration of salts in the soil, which can damage or kill crops.

subsidies government payments to farmers to encourage production of cheap food.

subsistence farming families or small communities using land to grow food primarily for their own use.

synthetic meat protein from vegetable or other sources, like fungi, manufactured to resemble meat.

yield quantity of any crop produced per acre.

INDEX

Photographic Credits:

Cover and pages 6, 7, 9, 11, 15, 26-27 and 29 top: USDA Photos; pages 2-3, 4-5, 5, 13, 17, 25 and 26: The Hutchison Library; page 8: Spectrum Color Library; page 10: Marie-Helene Bradley; page 12: Planet Earth Pictures; pages 14, 24, 27, 29 bottom and 32: The J. Allan Cash Photo Library; pages 16-17, 18 and 34: Robert Harding Picture Library; page 19: Topham Picture Source; page 22-23: FAO Photos; pages 28, 30-31 and 33: Zefa.

PRINTED IN BELGIUM BY

proost

INTERNATIONAL BOOK PRODUCTION